Values, Units, and Colors

Eric A. Meyer

O'REILLY®

Beijing · Cambridge · Farnham · Köln · Sebastopol · Tokyo

Values, Units, and Colors
by Eric A. Meyer

Published by O'Reilly Media, Inc., 1005 Gravenstein Highway North, Sebastopol, CA 95472.

O'Reilly books may be purchased for educational, business, or sales promotional use. Online editions are also available for most titles (*http://my.safaribooksonline.com*). For more information, contact our corporate/institutional sales department: 800-998-9938 or *corporate@oreilly.com*.

Editors: Simon St. Laurent and Meghan Blanchette
Production Editor: Kristen Borg
Copyeditor: Rachel Leach
Proofreader: O'Reilly Production Services

Cover Designer: Karen Montgomery
Interior Designer: David Futato
Illustrator: Robert Romano

Revision History for the First Edition:

2012-09-25	First release
2012-10-26	Second release

See *http://oreilly.com/catalog/errata.csp?isbn=9781449342517* for release details.

ISBN: 978-1-449-34251-7

[LSI]

1350944608

Table of Contents

Preface

Conventions Used in This Book

The following typographical conventions are used in this book:

Italic
> Indicates new terms, URLs, email addresses, filenames, and file extensions.

`Constant width`
> Used for program listings, as well as within paragraphs to refer to program elements such as variable or function names, databases, data types, environment variables, statements, and keywords.

`Constant width bold`
> Shows commands or other text that should be typed literally by the user.

`Constant width italic`
> Shows text that should be replaced with user-supplied values or by values determined by context.

 This icon signifies a tip, suggestion, or general note.

 This icon indicates a warning or caution.

Using Code Examples

This book is here to help you get your job done. In general, you may use the code in this book in your programs and documentation. You do not need to contact us for permission unless you're reproducing a significant portion of the code. For example, writing a program that uses several chunks of code from this book does not require permission. Selling or distributing a CD-ROM of examples from O'Reilly books does require permission. Answering a question by citing this book and quoting example code does not require permission. Incorporating a significant amount of example code from this book into your product's documentation does require permission.

We appreciate, but do not require, attribution. An attribution usually includes the title, author, publisher, and ISBN. For example: "*Values, Units, and Colors* by Eric A. Meyer (O'Reilly). Copyright 2012 O'Reilly Media, Inc., 978-1-449-34251-7."

If you feel your use of code examples falls outside fair use or the permission given above, feel free to contact us at *permissions@oreilly.com*.

Safari® Books Online

Safari Books Online (*www.safaribooksonline.com*) is an on-demand digital library that delivers expert content in both book and video form from the world's leading authors in technology and business.

Technology professionals, software developers, web designers, and business and creative professionals use Safari Books Online as their primary resource for research, problem solving, learning, and certification training.

Safari Books Online offers a range of product mixes and pricing programs for organizations, government agencies, and individuals. Subscribers have access to thousands of books, training videos, and prepublication manuscripts in one fully searchable database from publishers like O'Reilly Media, Prentice Hall Professional, Addison-Wesley Professional, Microsoft Press, Sams, Que, Peachpit Press, Focal Press, Cisco Press, John Wiley & Sons, Syngress, Morgan Kaufmann, IBM Redbooks, Packt, Adobe Press, FT Press, Apress, Manning, New Riders, McGraw-Hill, Jones & Bartlett, Course Technology, and dozens more. For more information about Safari Books Online, please visit us online.

How to Contact Us

Please address comments and questions concerning this book to the publisher:

O'Reilly Media, Inc.
1005 Gravenstein Highway North
Sebastopol, CA 95472
800-998-9938 (in the United States or Canada)
707-829-0515 (international or local)
707-829-0104 (fax)

We have a web page for this book, where we list errata, examples, and any additional information. You can access this page at *http://oreil.ly/values-units-colors*.

To comment or ask technical questions about this book, send email to *bookquestions@oreilly.com*.

For more information about our books, courses, conferences, and news, see our website at *http://www.oreilly.com*.

Find us on Facebook: *http://facebook.com/oreilly*

Follow us on Twitter: *http://twitter.com/oreillymedia*

Watch us on YouTube: *http://www.youtube.com/oreillymedia*

Values, Units, and Colors

In this book, we'll tackle features that are the basis for almost everything you can do with CSS: the units that affect the colors, distances, and sizes of a whole host of properties, as well as the units that help to define those values. Without units, you couldn't declare that an image should have 10 pixels of blank space around it, or that a heading's text should be a certain size. By understanding the concepts put forth here, you'll be able to learn and use the rest of CSS much more quickly.

Keywords, Strings, and Other Text Values

Of course, everything in a style sheet is text, but there are certain value types that directly represent strings of text as opposed to, say, numbers or colors. Included in this category are URLs and, interestingly enough, images.

Keywords

For those times when a value needs to be described with a word of some kind, there are *keywords*. A very common example is the keyword none, which is distinct from 0 (zero). Thus, to remove the underline from links in an HTML document, you would write:

```
a:link, a:visited {text-decoration: none;}
```

Similarly, if you want to force underlines on the links, then you would use the keyword underline.

If a property accepts keywords, then its keywords will be defined only for the scope of that property. If two properties use the same word as a keyword, the behavior of the keyword for one property will not necessarily be shared with the other. As an example, normal, as defined for letter-spacing, means something very different than the normal defined for font-style.

CSS3 defines two "global" keywords, one of which has fairly widespread support: inherit and initial.

inherit

The keyword `inherit` makes the value of a property on an element the same as the value of that property on its parent element. In other words, it forces inheritance to occur even in situations where it would not normally operate. In many cases, you don't need to specify inheritance, since many properties inherit naturally. Nevertheless, `inherit` can still be very useful.

For example, consider the following styles and markup:

```
#toolbar {background: blue; color: white;}

<div id="toolbar">
<a href="one.html">One</a> | <a href="two.html">Two</a> |
<a href="three.html">Three</a>
</div>
```

The `div` itself will have a blue background and a white foreground, but the links will be styled according to the browser's preference settings. They'll most likely end up as blue text on a blue background, with white vertical bars between them.

You could write a rule that explicitly sets the links in the "toolbar" to be white, but you can make things a little more robust by using `inherit`. You simply add the following rule to the style sheet:

```
#toolbar a {color: inherit;}
```

This will cause the links to use the inherited value of `color` in place of the user agent's default styles. Ordinarily, directly assigned styles override inherited styles, but `inherit` can undo that behavior.

Similarly, you can pull a property value down from a parent even if it wouldn't happen normally. Take `border`, for example, which is (rightfully) not inherited. If you want a `span` to inherit the border of its parent, all you need is `span {border: inherit;}`. More likely, though, you just want the border on a `span` to use the same border color as its parent. In that case `span {border-color: inherit;}` will do the trick.

 Internet Explorer did not support `inherit` until IE8.

initial

The keyword `initial` sets the value of a property to the defined initial value, which in a way means it "resets" the value. For example, the default value of `font-weight` is normal. Thus, declaring `font-weight: initial` is the same as declaring `font-weight: normal`.

This might seem a little bit silly until you consider that not all values have explicitly defined initial values. For example, the initial value for `color` is "depends on user agent." That's not a funky keyword you should type! What it means is that the default value of `color` depends on things like the preferences settings in a browser. While almost nobody changes the default text color setting from black, someone might set it to a dark gray or even a bright red. By declaring `color: initial;`, you're telling the browser to set the color of the element to whatever the user's default color is set to be.

 As of mid-2012, there was limited browser support for `initial`: Safari and Chrome supported it as-is, whereas Firefox supported it as `-moz-initial`.

Strings

A *string value* is an arbitrary sequence of characters wrapped in either single or double quotes, and is represented in value definitions with `<string>`. Two simple examples:

```
"I like to play with strings."
'Strings are fun to play with.'
```

Note that the quotes balance, which is to say that you always start and end with the same kind of quotes. Getting this wrong can lead to all kinds of parsing problems, since starting with one kind of quote and trying to end with the other means the string won't actually be terminated. You could accidentally incorporate following rules into the string that way!

If you want to put quote marks inside strings, that's okay as long as they're either not the kind you used to enclose the string or are escaped using a backslash.

```
"I've always liked to play with strings."
'He said to me, "I like to play with strings."'
"It's been said that \"haste makes waste.\""
'There\'s never been a "string theory" that I\'ve liked.'
```

Note that the only acceptable string delimiters are ' and ", sometimes called "straight quotes." That means you can't use "curly" or "smart" quotes to begin or end a string value. You can use them inside a string value, though, and they don't have to be escaped.

```
"It's been said that "haste makes waste.""
'There's never been a "string theory" that I've liked.'
```

Of course, this requires that you use Unicode encoding for your documents, but you should be doing that regardless.

If you have some reason to include a newline in your string value, you can do that by escaping the newline itself. CSS will then remove it, making things as if it had never been there. Thus, the following two string values are identical from a CSS point of view:

```
"This is the right place \
for a newline."
"This is the right place for a newline."
```

If, on the other hand, you actually want a string value that includes a newline character, then use the Unicode reference \A where you want the newline to occur.

```
"This is a better place \Afor a newline."
```

URLs

If you've written web pages, you're obviously familiar with URLs (or, as in CSS2.1, URIs). Whenever you need to refer to one—as in the @import statement, which is used when importing an external style sheet—the general format is:

```
url(protocol://server/pathname)
```

This example defines what is known as an *absolute URL*. By absolute, I mean a URL that will work no matter where (or rather, in what page) it's found, because it defines an absolute location in web space. Let's say that you have a server called web.waffles.org (*http://web.waffles.org*). On that server, there is a directory called `pix`, and in this directory is an image *waffle22.gif*. In this case, the absolute URL of that image would be:

```
http://web.waffles.org/pix/waffle22.gif
```

This URL is valid no matter where it is found, whether the page that contains it is located on the server *web.waffles.org* or *web.pancakes.com*.

The other type of URL is a *relative URL*, so named because it specifies a location that is relative to the document that uses it. If you're referring to a relative location, such as a file in the same directory as your web page, then the general format is:

```
url(pathname)
```

This works only if the image is on the same server as the page that contains the URL. For argument's sake, assume that you have a web page located at *http://web.waffles.org/syrup.html* and that you want the image *waffle22.gif* to appear on this page. In that case, the URL would be:

```
pix/waffle22.gif
```

This path works because the web browser knows that it should start with the place it found the web document and then add the relative URL. In this case, the pathname *pix/waffle22.gif* added to the server name *http://web.waffles.org* equals *http://web.waffles.org/pix/waffle22.gif*. You can almost always use an absolute URL in place of a relative URL; it doesn't matter which you use, as long as it defines a valid location.

In CSS, relative URLs are relative to the style sheet itself, not to the HTML document that uses the style sheet. For example, you may have an external style sheet that imports another style sheet. If you use a relative URL to import the second style sheet, it must be relative to the first style sheet.

As an example, consider an HTML document at *http://web.waffles.org/toppings/tips .html*, which has a link to the style sheet *http://web.waffles.org/styles/basic.css*:

```
<link rel="stylesheet" type="text/css"
    href="http://web.waffles.org/styles/basic.css">
```

Inside the file *basic.css* is an @import statement referring to another style sheet:

```
@import url(special/toppings.css);
```

This @import will cause the browser to look for the style sheet at *http://web.waffles.org/ styles/special/toppings.css*, not at *http://web.waffles.org/toppings/special/toppings.css*. If you have a style sheet at the latter location, then the @import in *basic.css* should read:

```
@import url(http://web.waffles.org/toppings/special/toppings.css);
```

Note that there cannot be a space between the url and the opening parenthesis:

```
body {background: url(http://www.pix.web/picture1.jpg);}   /* correct */
body {background: url  (images/picture2.jpg);}        /* INCORRECT */
```

If the space is present, the entire declaration will be invalidated and thus ignored.

Images

An *image value* is a reference to an image, as you might have guessed. Its syntax representation is *<image>*.

At the most basic level of support, which his to say the one every CSS engine on the planet would understand, an *<image>* value is simply a *<url>* value. In more advanced user agents, *<image>* stands for one of the following:

<url>
> A URL identifier of an external resource; in this case, the URL of an image.

<image-list>
> Perhaps unsurprisingly, a list of images. As of mid-2012 there was no support for this value type.

<element-reference>
> Refers to an element within the document. The element is then copied and used as an image, possibly as a "live" copy—that is to say, a copy that updates if the element is altered through Dom scripting or user interaction. As of mid-2012, only Firefox supported this capability.

<gradient>
> Refers to either a linear or radial gradient image. Gradients are fairly complex.

Identifiers

There are a few properties that accept an *identifier value*, which is a user-defined identifier of some kind; the most common example is generated list counters. They are represented in the value syntax as `<identifier>`. Identifiers themselves are strings, and are case-sensitive; thus, `myID` and `MyID` are, as far as CSS is concerned, completely distinct and unrelated to each other. In cases where a property accepts both an identifier and one or more keywords, the user cannot define an identifier identical to a valid keyword.

Numbers and Percentages

These value types are special because they serve as the foundation for so many other values types. For example, font sizes can be defined using the `em` identifier (covered later in this text) preceded by a number. But what kind of number? Defining the types of numbers here lets us speak clearly later on.

Integers

An *integer value* is about as simple as it gets: one or more numbers, optionally prefixed by a + or - sign to indicate a positive or negative value. That's it. Integer values are represented in value syntax as `<integer>`. Examples include 13, –42, 712, and 1066.

Integer values that fall outside a defined range are, by default, considered invalid and cause the entire declaration to be ignored. However, some properties define behavior that causes values outside the accepted range to be set to the accepted value closest to the declared value. In cases (such as the property `z-index`) where there is no restricted range, user agents must support values up to $\pm 1,073,741,824$ ($\pm 2^{30}$).

Numbers

A *number value* is either an `<integer>` or a real number, which is to say an integer followed by a dot and then some number of following integers. Additionally, it can be prefixed by either + or - to indicate positive or negative values. Number values are represented in value syntax as `<number>`. Examples include 2.7183, –3.1416, and 6.2832.

The reason a `<number>` can be an `<integer>` and yet there are separate value types is that some properties will only accept integers (e.g., `z-index`), whereas others will accept any real number (e.g., `opacity`). As with integer values, number values may have limits imposed on them by a property definition; for example, `opacity` restricts its value to be any valid `<number>` in the range 0 to 1, inclusive. As with integers, number values that fall outside a defined range are, by default, considered invalid and cause the entire declaration to be ignored. However, some properties define behavior that causes values outside the accepted range to be set to the accepted value closest to the declared value.

Percentages

A *percentage value* is a *<number>* followed by a percentage sign (%), and is represented in value syntax as *<percentage>*. Examples would include 50% and 33.333%. Percentage values are always relative to another value, which can be anything—the value of another property of the same element, a value inherited from the parent element, or a value of an ancestor element. Any property that accepts percentage values will define any restrictions on the range of allowed percentage values, and will also define the way in which the percentage is relatively calculated.

Distances

Many CSS properties, such as margins, depend on length measurements to properly display various page elements. It's no surprise, then, that there are a number of ways to measure length in CSS.

All length units can be expressed as either positive or negative numbers followed by a label (although some properties will accept only positive numbers). You can also use real numbers—that is, numbers with decimal fractions, such as 10.5 or 4.561. All length units are followed by short abbreviation (usually two characters) that represents the actual unit of length being specified, such as in (inches) or pt (points). The only exception to this rule is a length of 0 (zero), which need not be followed by a unit.

These length units are divided into two types: *absolute length units* and *relative length units*.

Absolute Length Units

We'll start with absolute units because they're easiest to understand, despite the fact that they're almost unusable in regular web design. The six types of absolute units are as follows:

Inches (in)
> As you might expect, this notation refers to the inches you'd find on a ruler in the United States. (The fact that this unit is in the specification, even though almost the entire world uses the metric system, is an interesting insight into the pervasiveness of U.S. interests on the Internet—but let's not get into virtual sociopolitical theory right now.)

Centimeters (cm)
> Refers to the centimeters that you'd find on rulers the world over. There are 2.54 centimeters to an inch, and one centimeter equals 0.394 inches.

Millimeters (mm)
> For those Americans who are metric-challenged, there are 10 millimeters to a centimeter, so an inch equals 25.4 millimeters, and a millimeter equals 0.0394 inches.

Points (pt)

Points are standard typographical measurements that have been used by printers and typesetters for decades and by word processing programs for many years. Traditionally, there are 72 points to an inch (points were defined before widespread use of the metric system). Therefore, the capital letters of text set to 12 points should be one-sixth of an inch tall. For example, p {font-size: 18pt;} is equivalent to p {font-size: 0.25in;}.

Picas (pc)

Picas are another typographical term. A pica is equivalent to 12 points, which means there are 6 picas to an inch. As just shown, the capital letters of text set to 1 pica should be one-sixth of an inch tall. For example, p {font-size: 1.5pc;} would set text to the same size as the example declarations found in the definition of points.

Pixels (px)

A pixel is a small box on screen, but CSS defines pixels more abstractly. In CSS terms, a pixel is defined to be the size required to yield 96 pixels per inch. Many user agents ignore this definition in favor of simply addressing the pixels on the monitor. Scaling factors are brought into play when page zooming or printing, where an element 100px wide can be rendered more than 100 device dots wide.

Of course, these units are really useful only if the browser knows all the details of the monitor on which your page is displayed, the printer you're using, or whatever other user agent might apply. On a web browser, display is affected by the size of the monitor and the resolution to which the monitor is set—and there isn't much that you, as the author, can do about these factors. You can only hope that, if nothing else, the measurements will be consistent in relation to each other—that is, that a setting of 1.0in will be twice as large as 0.5in, as shown in Figure 1.

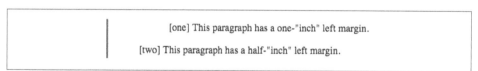

[one] This paragraph has a one-"inch" left margin.

[two] This paragraph has a half-"inch" left margin.

Figure 1. Setting absolute-length left margins

Nevertheless, despite all that, let's make the highly suspect assumption that your computer knows enough about its display system to accurately reproduce real-world measurements. In that case, you could make sure every paragraph has a top margin of half an inch by declaring p {margin-top: 0.5in;}. Regardless of font size or any other circumstances, a paragraph will have a half-inch top margin.

Absolute units are much more useful in defining style sheets for printed documents, where measuring things in terms of inches, points, and picas is much more common.

Pixel lengths

On the face of things, pixels are straightforward. If you look at a monitor closely enough, you can see that it's broken up into a grid of tiny little boxes. Each box is a pixel. If you define an element to be a certain number of pixels tall and wide, as in the following markup:

```
<p>
The following image is 20 pixels tall and wide: <img src="test.gif"
   style="width: 20px; height: 20px;" alt="" />
</p>
```

...then it follows that the element will be that many monitor elements tall and wide, as shown in Figure 2.

Figure 2. Using pixel lengths

In general, if you declare something like font-size: 18px, a web browser will almost certainly use actual pixels on your monitor—after all, they're already there—but with other display devices, like printers, the user agent will have to rescale pixel lengths to something more sensible. In other words, the printing code has to figure out how many dots there are in a pixel.

Unfortunately, there is a potential drawback to using pixels. If you set font sizes in pixels, then users of Internet Explorer for Windows previous to IE7 cannot resize the text using the Text Size menu in their browser. This can be a problem if your text is too small for a user to comfortably read. If you use more flexible measurements, such as em, the user can resize text. (If you're exceedingly protective of your design, you might call *that* a drawback, of course.)

 One example of a problem with pixel measurements can be found in an early CSS1 implementation. In Internet Explorer 3.x, when a document was printed, IE3 assumed that 18px was the same as 18 dots, which on a 600dpi printer works out to be 18/600, or 3/100, of an inch—or, if you prefer, .03in. That's pretty small text!

On the other hand, pixel measurements are perfect for expressing the size of images, which are already a certain number of pixels tall and wide. In fact, the only time you would not want pixels to express image size is when you want them scaled along with the size of the text. This is an admirable and sometimes useful approach. You do end up relying on the image-scaling routines in user agents, but those have been getting pretty good. Scaling of images *really* makes sense with vector-based images like SVG, of course.

Pixel theory

In its discussion of pixels, the CSS specification recommends that in cases where a display type is significantly different than 96 pixels per inch (ppi), user agents should scale pixel measurements to a "reference pixel." CSS2 recommended 90ppi as the reference pixel, but CSS2.1 and CSS3 recommend 96ppi. The most common example is a printer, which has dots instead of pixels, and which has a lot more dots per inch than 96! In printing web content, then, it may assume 96 pixels per inch and scale its output accordingly.

If a display's resolution is set to 1,024 pixels wide by 768 pixels tall, its screen size is exactly ten and two-thirds inches wide by eight inches tall, and the screen it is filled entirely by the display pixels, then each pixel will be 1/96 of an inch wide and tall. As you might guess, this scenario is a fairly rare occurrence. So, on most displays, the actual number of pixels per inch (ppi) is higher than 96—sometimes much higher. The Retina display on an iPhone 4S, for example, is 326ppi; the display on the iPad 3,264ppi.

 As a Windows 7 user, you should be able to set your display driver to make the display of elements correspond correctly to real-world measurements. To do so, click Start→Control Panel. In the Control Panel click Display; then click "Set custom text size (DPI)" in the left sidebar; then hold a ruler up to the screen and move the slider until the onscreen ruler matches the physical ruler. Click OK until you're free of dialog boxes, and you're set.

In Windows XP, the path to the ruler dialog is Start→Control Panel; double-click Display; click the Settings tab; then click Advanced to reveal a dialog box (which may differ on each PC). You should see a drop-down or other form control labeled "Font Size;" select "Other."

Resolution Units

With the advent of media queries, three new unit types were introduced in order to be able to describe display resolution:

Dots per inch (dpi)
> The number of display dots per linear inch. This can refer to the dots in a paper printer's output, the physical pixels in an LED monitor or other device, or the elements in an e-ink display such as that used by a Kindle.

Dots per centimeter (dpcm)
> Same as dpi, except the linear measure is one centimeter instead of one inch.

Dots per pixel unit (dppx)
> The number of display dots per CSS px unit, as described previously. As of CSS3, 1dppx is equivalent to 96dpi because CSS defines pixel units at that ratio. Of course, that ratio could change in future versions of CSS.

As of mid-2012, these units are only used in the context of media queries. As an example, an author can set a media block to be used only on displays that have higher than 500dpi:

```
@media (min-resolution: 500dpi) {...}
```

Interestingly, **dppx** is not defined by the Media Queries module, but appears in the Units and Values modules alongside **dpi** and **dpcm**, which are defined in Media Queries. What this means for the future is by no means clear.

Relative Length Units

Relative units are so called because they are measured in relation to other things. The actual (or absolute) distance they measure can change due to factors beyond their control, such as screen resolution, the width of the viewing area, the user's preference settings, and a whole host of other things. In addition, for some relative units, their size is almost always relative to the element that uses them and will thus change from element to element.

em and ex units

First, let's consider **em** and **ex**, which are closely related. In CSS, one "em" is defined to be the value of **font-size** for a given font. If the **font-size** of an element is 14 pixels, then for that element, **1em** is equal to 14 pixels.

Obviously, this value can change from element to element. For example, let's say you have an **h1** with a font size of 24 pixels, an **h2** element with a font size of 18 pixels, and a paragraph with a font size of 12 pixels. If you set the left margin of all three at **1em**, they will have left margins of 24 pixels, 18 pixels, and 12 pixels, respectively:

```
h1 {font-size: 24px;}
h2 {font-size: 18px;}
p {font-size: 12px;}
h1, h2, p {margin-left: 1em;}
small {font-size: 0.8em;}

<h1>Left margin = <small>24 pixels</small></h1>
<h2>Left margin = <small>18 pixels</small></h2>
<p>Left margin = <small>12 pixels</small></p>
```

When setting the size of the font, on the other hand, the value of **em** is relative to the font size of the parent element, as illustrated by Figure 3.

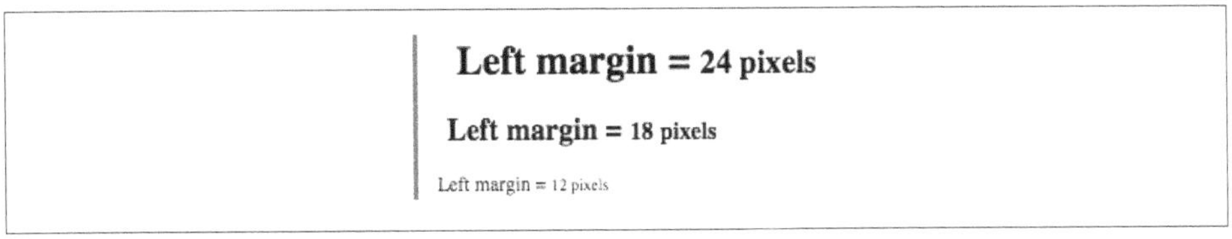

Figure 3. Using em for margins and font sizing

In theory, one "em" is equal to the width of a lowercase "m" in the font used—that's where the name comes from, in fact. It's an old typographer's term. However, this is not assured in CSS.

ex, on the other hand, refers to the height of a lowercase x in the font being used. Therefore, if you have two paragraphs in which the text is 24 points in size, but each paragraph uses a different font, then the value of ex could be different for each paragraph. This is because different fonts have different heights for x, as you can see in Figure 4. Even though the examples use 24-point text—and therefore, each example's em value is 24 points—the x-height for each is different.

Times: x

Garamond: x

Helvetica: x

Arial: x

Impact: x

Courier: x

Figure 4. Varying x-heights

The rem unit

Like the em unit, the rem unit is based on declared font size. The difference—and it's a doozy—is that whereas em is calculated using the font size of the element to which it's applied, rem is *always* calculated using the root element. In HTML, that's the html element. Thus, declaring any element to have font-size: 1rem; is setting it to have the same font-size value as the root element of the document.

As an example, consider the following markup fragment. It will have the result shown in Figure 5.

```
<p> This paragraph has the same font size as the root element thanks to inheritance.</p>
<div style="font-size: 30px; background: silver;">
  <p style="font-size: 1em;">This paragraph has the same font size as its parent
element.</p>
  <p style="font-size: 1rem;">This paragraph has the same font size as the root
element.</p>
</div>
```

This paragraph has the same font size as the root element thanks to inheritance.

This paragraph has the same font size as its parent element.

This paragraph has the same font size as the root element.

Figure 5. ems versus rems

Basically, rem acts as a reset for font size: no matter what relative font sizing has happened to the ancestors of an element, giving it font-size: 1rem; will put it right back where the root element is set. This will usually be the user's default font size, unless of course you (or the user) have set the root element to a specific font size.

For example, given this declaration, 1rem will always be equivalent to 13px:

```
html {font-size: 13px;}
```

However, given *this* declaration, 1rem will always be equivalent to three-quarters the user's default font size:

```
html {font-size: 75%;}
```

In this case, if the user's default is 16 pixels, then 1rem will equal 12px. If the user has actually set their default to 12 pixels—a few people do this—then 1rem will equal 9px; if the default setting is 20 pixels, then 1rem equals 15px. And so on.

Of course, you are not restricted to the value 1rem. Any real number can be used, just as with the em unit, so you can do fun things like set all of your headings to be multiples of the root element's font size:

```
h1 {font-size: 2rem;}
h2 {font-size: 1.75rem;}
h3 {font-size: 1.4rem;}
h4 {font-size: 1.1rem;}
h5 {font-size: 1rem;}
h6 {font-size: 0.8rem;}
```

 As of mid-2012, support for rem was fairly widespread, missing only in older versions of browsers that could still be hanging around.

The ch unit

An interesting addition to CSS3 is the ch unit, which is broadly meant to represent "one character." The way it is defined in CSS3 is:

> Equal to the advance measure of the "0" (ZERO, U+0030) glyph found in the font used to render it.

The term "advance measure" is actually a CSS-ism that corresponds to the term "advance width" in font typography. (CSS uses the term "measure" because some scripts are not right-to-left or left-to-right, and so may have an advance height rather than an advance width.) Without getting into too many details, a character glyph's advance width is the distance from the start of a character glyph to the start of the next. This generally corresponds to the width of the glyph itself plus any built-in spacing to the sides. (Although that built-in spacing can be either positive or negative.)

As mentioned previously, CSS pins the ch unit to the advance width of a zero in a given font. This is in parallel to the way that em is calculated with respect to the font-size value of an element.

The easiest way to demonstrate this unit is to run a bunch of zeroes together and then set an image to have a width with the same number of ch units as the number of zeroes, as shown in Figure 6.

```
img {height: 1em; width: 25ch;}
```

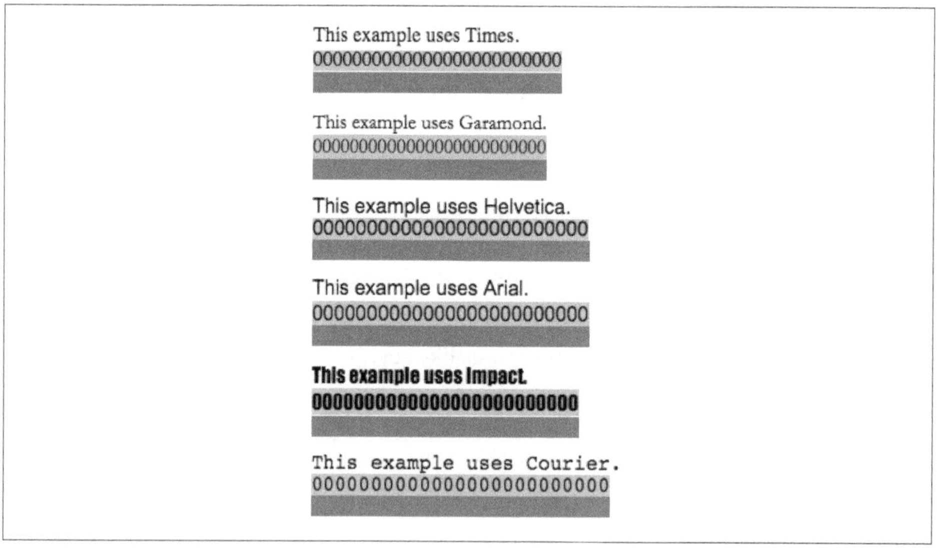

Figure 6. Character-relative sizing

Given a monospace font, all characters are by definition 1ch wide. In any proportional face type, which is what the vast majority of Western typefaces are, characters may be wider or narrower than the "0" and so cannot be assumed to be 1ch wide.

 As of mid-2012, support for ch was limited to Firefox.

Viewport-relative units

Another new addition in CSS3 are the three viewport-relative size units. These are calculated with respect to the size of the viewport—browser window, printable area, mobile device display, etc.

Viewport width unit (vw)
> This unit is calculated with respect to the viewport's width, which is divided by 100. Therefore, if the viewport is 937 pixels wide, 1vw is equal to 9.37px. If the viewport's width changes, say by dragging the browser window wider or more narrow, the value of vw changes along with it.

Viewport height unit (vh)
> This unit is calculated with respect to the viewport's height, which is divided by 100. Therefore, if the viewport is 650 pixels tall, 1vh is equal to 6.5px. If the viewport's height changes, say by dragging the browser window taller or shorter, the value of vh changes along with it.

Viewport minimum unit (vmin)
> This unit is 1/100 of the viewport's width or height, whichever is *lesser*. Thus, given a viewport that is 937 pixels wide by 650 pixels tall, 1vmin is equal to 6.5px.

These units are particularly handy for creating full-viewport interfaces, such as those one would expect to find on a mobile device, because it can allow elements to be sized compared to the viewport and not any of the elements within the document tree. It's thus very simple to fill up the entire viewport, or at least major portions of it, and not have to worry about the precise dimensions of the actual viewport in any particular case.

Here's a very basic example of viewport-relative sizing, which is illustrated in Figure 7.

```
div {width: 50vh; height: 33vw; background: gray;}
```

An interesting (though perhaps not useful) fact about these units is that they aren't bound to their own primary axis. Thus, for example, you can declare width: 25vh; to make an element as wide as one-quarter the height of the viewport.

 As of mid-2012, support for these units was limited to Internet Explorer 9 and above.

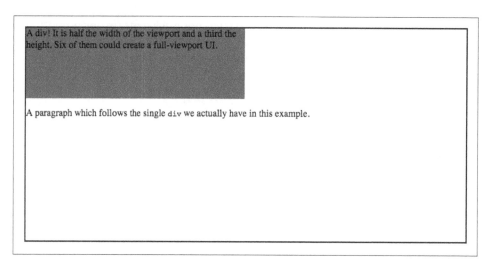

Figure 7. Viewport-relative sizing

Color

One of the first questions every starting web author asks is, "How do I set colors on my page?" Under HTML, you have two choices: you could use one of a small number of colors with names, such as **red** or **purple**, or employ a vaguely cryptic method using hexadecimal codes. Both of these methods for describing colors remain in CSS, along with some other—and, I think, more intuitive—methods.

Named Colors

Assuming that you're content to pick from a small, basic set of colors, the easiest method is simply to use the name of the color you want. CSS calls these color choices, logically enough, *named colors*. As of CSS3, the CSS color specification defines 16 basic color keywords, which are the 16 colors defined in HTML 4.01, as shown in Table 1.

Table 1. The basic 16 color keywords

aqua	gray	navy	silver
black	green	olive	teal
blue	lime	purple	white
fuchsia	maroon	red	yellow

So, let's say you want all first-level headings to be maroon. The best declaration would be:

```
h1 {color: maroon;}
```

Simple and straightforward, isn't it? Figure 8 shows a few more examples:

```
h1 {color: silver;}
h2 {color: fuchsia;}
h3 {color: navy;}
```

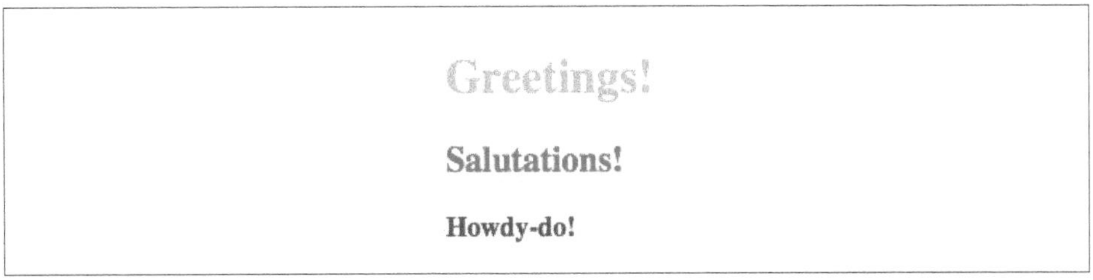

Greetings!

Salutations!

Howdy-do!

Figure 8. Naming colors

Of course, you've probably seen (and maybe even used) color names other than the ones listed earlier. For example, if you specify:

```
h1 {color: lightgreen;}
```

As of the CSS3 color specification, the 16 colors from HTML 4.01 have been subsumed into a longer list of 147 color keywords. This extended list is based on the standard X11 RGB values that have been in use for decades, and have been recognized by browsers for many years, with the addition of some color names from SVG (mostly involving variants of "gray" and "grey"). A table of color equivalents for all 147 keywords defined in the CSS Color Module Level 3 is given in "Color Equivalence Table" on page 28.

Fortunately, there are more detailed and precise ways to specify colors in CSS. The advantage is that, with these methods, you can specify any color in the color spectrum, not just 17 (or 140) named colors.

Colors by RGB and RGBa

Computers create colors by combining different levels of red, green, and blue, a combination that is often referred to as *RGB color*. Each point of display is known as a pixel, which is a term discussed earlier in the chapter. Given the way colors are created on a monitor, it makes sense that you should have direct access to those colors, determining your own mixture of the three for maximum control. That solution is complex, but possible, and the payoffs are worth it because there are very few limits on which colors you can produce. There are four ways to affect color in this manner.

Functional RGB colors

There are two color value types that use *functional RGB notation* as opposed to hexadecimal notation. The generic syntax for this type of color value is `rgb(color)`, where `color` is expressed using a triplet of either percentages or integers. The percentage values can be in the range 0%–100%, and the integers can be in the range 0–255.

Thus, to specify white and black, respectively, using percentage notation, the values would be:

```
rgb(100%,100%,100%)
rgb(0%,0%,0%)
```

Using the integer-triplet notation, the same colors would be represented as:

```
rgb(255,255,255)
rgb(0,0,0)
```

Assume you want your h1 elements to be a shade of red that lies between the values for red and maroon. red is equivalent to rgb(100%,0%,0%), whereas maroon is equal to (50%, 0%,0%). To get a color between those two, you might try this:

```
h1 {color: rgb(75%,0%,0%);}
```

This makes the red component of the color lighter than maroon, but darker than red. If, on the other hand, you want to create a pale red color, you would raise the green and blue levels:

```
h1 {color: rgb(75%,50%,50%);}
```

The closest equivalent color using integer-triplet notation is:

```
h1 {color: rgb(191,127,127);}
```

The easiest way to visualize how these values correspond to color is to create a table of gray values. The result is shown in Figure 9:

```
p.one {color: rgb(0%,0%,0%);}
p.two {color: rgb(20%,20%,20%);}
p.three {color: rgb(40%,40%,40%);}
p.four {color: rgb(60%,60%,60%);}
p.five {color: rgb(80%,80%,80%);}
p.six {color: rgb(0,0,0);}
p.seven {color: rgb(51,51,51);}
p.eight {color: rgb(102,102,102);}
p.nine {color: rgb(153,153,153);}
p.ten {color: rgb(204,204,204);}
```

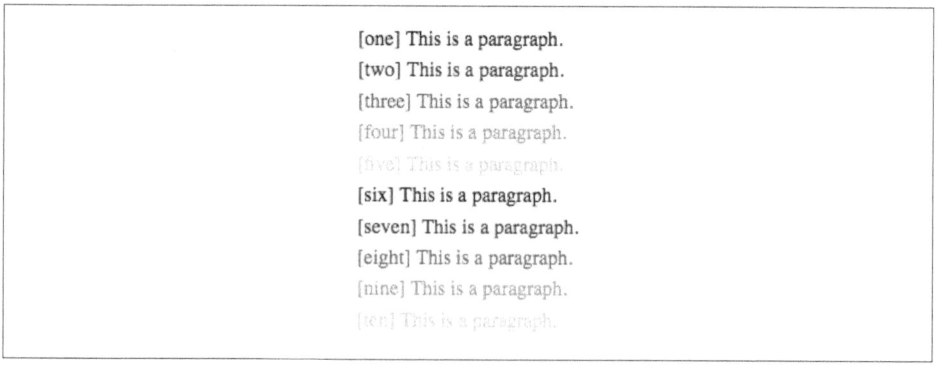

[one] This is a paragraph.

[two] This is a paragraph.

[three] This is a paragraph.

[four] This is a paragraph.

[five] This is a paragraph.

[six] This is a paragraph.

[seven] This is a paragraph.

[eight] This is a paragraph.

[nine] This is a paragraph.

[ten] This is a paragraph.

Figure 9. Text set in shades of gray

Of course, since we're dealing in shades of gray, all three RGB values are the same in each statement. If any one of them were different from the others, then a color hue would start to emerge. If, for example, rgb(50%,50%,50%) were modified to be rgb(50%, 50%,60%), the result would be a medium-dark color with just a hint of blue.

It is possible to use fractional numbers in percentage notation. You might, for some reason, want to specify that a color be exactly 25.5 percent red, 40 percent green, and 98.6 percent blue:

```
h2 {color: rgb(25.5%,40%,98.6%);}
```

A user agent that ignores the decimal points (and some do) should round the value to the nearest integer, resulting in a declared value of rgb(26%,40%,99%). In integer triplets, of course, you are limited to integers.

Values that fall outside the allowed range for each notation are "clipped" to the nearest range edge, meaning that a value that is greater than 100% or less than 0% will default to those allowed extremes. Thus, the following declarations would be treated as if they were the values indicated in the comments:

```
P.one {color: rgb(300%,4200%,110%);}    /*  100%,100%,100%  */
P.two {color: rgb(0%,-40%,-5000%);}     /*  0%,0%,0%  */
p.three {color: rgb(42,444,-13);}       /* 42,255,0  */
```

Conversion between percentages and integers may seem arbitrary, but there's no need to guess at the integer you want—there's a simple formula for calculating them. If you know the percentages for each of the RGB levels you want, then you need only apply them to the number 255 to get the resulting values. Let's say you have a color of 25 percent red, 37.5 percent green, and 60 percent blue. Multiply each of these percentages by 255, and you get 63.75, 95.625, and 153. Round these values to the nearest integers, and *voilà*: rgb(64,96,153).

Of course, if you already know the percentage values, there isn't much point in converting them into integers. Integer notation is more useful for people who use programs such as Photoshop, which can display integer values in the "Info" dialog, or for those who are so familiar with the technical details of color generation that they normally think in values of 0–255.

RGBa colors

As of CSS3, the two functional RGB notations were extended into a functional RGBa notation. This notation simply adds an alpha value to the end of the RGB triplets; thus, "red-green-blue-alpha" becomes RGBa. The alpha stands for *alpha channel*, which is a measure of opacity.

For example, suppose you wanted an element's text to be half-opaque white. That way, any background color behind the text would "shine through," mixing with the half-transparent white. You would write one of the following two values:

```
rgba(255,255,255,0.5)
rgba(100%,100%,100%,0.5)
```

To make a color completely transparent, you simply set the alpha value to 0; to be completely opaque, the correct value is 1. Thus, rgb(0,0,0) and rgba(0,0,0,1) will yield precisely the same result (black). Figure 10 shows a series of paragraphs set in increasingly transparent black, which is the result of the following rules.

```
p.one {color: rgba(0,0,0,1);}
p.two {color: rgba(0%,0%,0%,0.8);}
p.three {color: rgba(0,0,0,0.6);}
p.four {color: rgba(0%,0%,0%,0.4);}
p.five {color: rgba(0,0,0,0.2);}
```

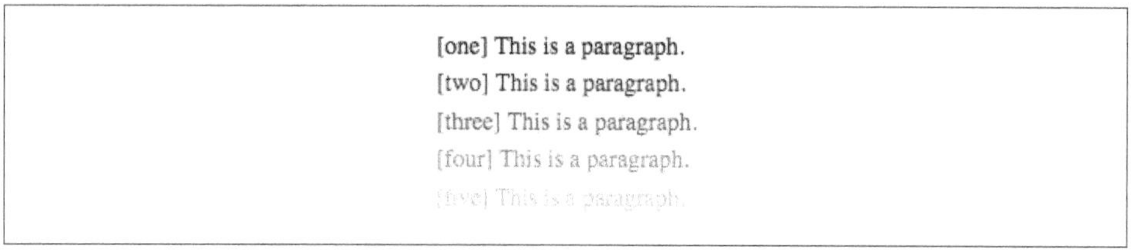

[one] This is a paragraph.

[two] This is a paragraph.

[three] This is a paragraph.

[four] This is a paragraph.

[five] This is a paragraph.

Figure 10. Text set in progressive translucency

As you've no doubt already inferred, alpha values are always real numbers in the range 0 to 1. Any value outside that range will either be ignored or reset to the nearest valid alpha value. You cannot use *‹percentage›* to represent alpha values, despite the mathematical equivalence.

Hexadecimal RGB colors

CSS allows you to define a color using the same hexadecimal color notation so familiar to old-school HTML web authors:

```
h1 {color: #FF0000;}   /* set H1s to red */
h2 {color: #903BC0;}   /* set H2s to a dusky purple */
h3 {color: #000000;}   /* set H3s to black */
h4 {color: #808080;}   /* set H4s to medium gray */
```

Computers have been using "hex notation" for quite some time now, and programmers are typically either trained in its use or pick it up through experience. Their familiarity with hexadecimal notation likely led to its use in setting colors in HTML. The practice was simply carried over to CSS.

Here's how it works: by stringing together three hexadecimal numbers in the range 00 through FF, you can set a color. The generic syntax for this notation is #RRGGBB. Note that there are no spaces, commas, or other separators between the three numbers.

Hexadecimal notation is mathematically equivalent to the integer-pair notation discussed in the previous section. For example, rgb(255,255,255) is precisely equivalent to #FFFFFF, and rgb(51,102,128) is the same as #336680. Feel free to use whichever notation you prefer—it will be rendered identically by most user agents. If you have a calculator that converts between decimal and hexadecimal, making the jump from one to the other should be pretty simple.

For hexadecimal numbers that are composed of three matched pairs of digits, CSS permits a shortened notation. The generic syntax of this notation is #RGB:

```
h1 {color: #000;}   /* set H1s to black */
h2 {color: #666;}   /* set H2s to dark gray */
h3 {color: #FFF;}   /* set H3s to white */
```

As you can see from the markup, there are only three digits in each color value. However, since hexadecimal numbers between 00 and FF need two digits each, and you have only three total digits, how does this method work?

The answer is that the browser takes each digit and replicates it. Therefore, #F00 is equivalent to #FF0000, #6FA would be the same as #66FFAA, and #FFF would come out #FFFFFF, which is the same as white. Obviously, not every color can be represented in this manner. Medium gray, for example, would be written in standard hexadecimal notation as #808080. This cannot be expressed in shorthand; the closest equivalent would be #888, which is the same as #888888.

There is no hexadecimal notation that includes alpha values.

Colors by HSL and HSLa

New to CSS3 (though not to the world of color theory in general) are HSL notations. HSL stands for **H**ue, **S**aturation, and **L**ightness, where the hue is a hue angle in the range 0–360, saturation is a percentage value from 0 (no saturation) to 100 (full saturation), and lightness is a percentage value from 0 (completely dark) to 100 (completely light).

The hue angle is expressed in terms of a circle around which the full spectrum of colors progresses. It starts with red at zero degrees and then proceeds through the rainbow until it comes to red again at 360 degrees. Figure 11 illustrates this visually by showing the angles and colors of the spectrum on a wheel as well as a linear strip.

If you're intimately familiar with RGB, then HSL may be confusing at first. (But then, RGB is confusing for people familiar with HSL.) You may be able to better grasp the hues in HSL by contemplating the diagram in Figure 12, which shows the spectrum results from placing and then mixing red, green, and blue.

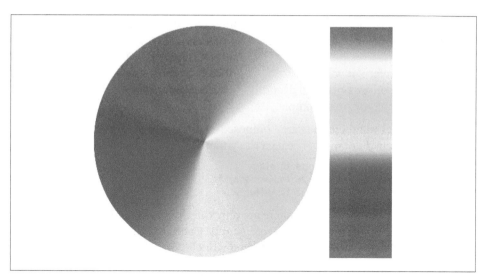

Figure 11. The spectrum on a wheel and a strip

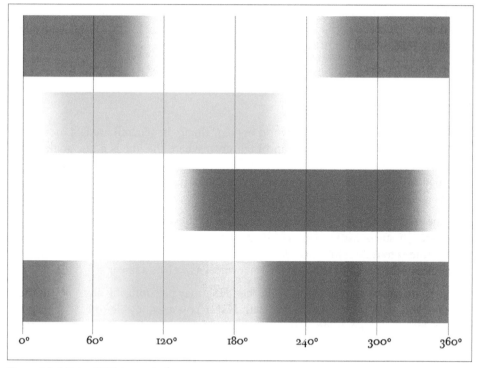

0°   60°   120°   180°   240°   300°   360°

Figure 12. Mixing RGB to create the spectrum

As for the other two values, saturation measures the intensity of a color. A saturation of 0% always yields a shade of gray, no matter what hue angle you have set, and a saturation of 100% creates the most vivid shade of that hue for a given lightness. Similarly, lightness defines how dark or light the color appears. A lightness of 0% is always black, regardless of the other hue and saturation values, just as a lightness of 100% always yields white. Consider the results of the following styles, illustrated on the left side of Figure 13.

```
p.one {color: hsl(0,0%,0%);}
p.two{color: hsl(60,0%,25%);}
p.three {color: hsl(120,0%,50%);}
p.four {color: hsl(180,0%,75%);}
p.five {color: hsl(240,0%,0%);}
p.six {color: hsl(300,0%,25%);}
p.seven {color: hsl(360,0%,50%);}
```

[one] This paragraph's color has 0% saturation.	[one] This paragraph's color has 50% saturation.
[two] This paragraph's color has 0% saturation.	[two] This paragraph's color has 50% saturation.
[three] This paragraph's color has 0% saturation.	[three] This paragraph's color has 50% saturation.
[four] This paragraph's color has 0% saturation.	
[five] This paragraph's color has 0% saturation.	[five] This paragraph's color has 50% saturation.
[six] This paragraph's color has 0% saturation.	[six] This paragraph's color has 50% saturation.
[seven] This paragraph's color has 0% saturation.	[seven] This paragraph's color has 50% saturation.

Figure 13. Varying lightness and hues

The gray you see isn't just a function of the limitations of print: every single one of those bits of text is a shade of gray, because every color value has 0% in the saturation (middle) position. The degree of lightness or darkness is set by the lightness (third) position. In all seven examples, the hue angle changes, and in none of them does it matter. But that's only so long as the saturation remains at 0%. If that value is raised to, say, 50%, then the hue angle will become very important, because it will control what sort of color you see. Consider the same set of values that we saw before, but all set to 50% saturation, as illustrated on the right side of Figure 13.

It can be instructive to take the 16 color keywords defined in HTML4 (Table 1) and plot them against a hue-and-lightness wheel, as shown in Figure 14. The color wheel not only features the full spectrum around the rim, but also runs from 50 percent lightness at the edge to 0 percent lightness in the center. (The saturation is 100 percent throughout.) As you can see, the twelve keywords of color are regularly placed throughout the wheel, which bespeaks careful choice on the part of whoever chose them. The gray shades aren't quite as regularly placed, but are probably the most useful distribution of shades given that there were only four of them.

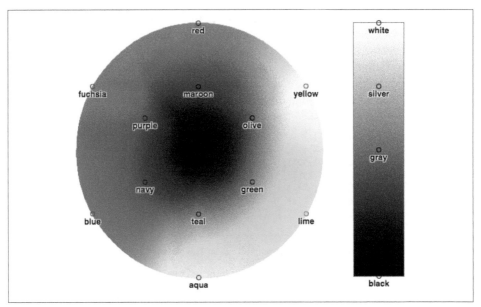

Figure 14. Keyword-equivalent hue angles and lightnesses

Just as RGB has its RGBa counterpart, HSL has an HSLa counterpart. This is simply an HSL triplet followed by an alpha value in the range 0–1. The following HSLa values are all black with varying shades of transparency, just as in the RGBa section earlier (and illustrated in Figure 10).

```
p.one {color: hsla(0,0%,0%,1);}
p.two {color: hsla(0,0%,0%,0.8);}
p.three {color: hsla(0,0%,0%,0.6);}
p.four {color: hsla(0,0%,0%,0.4);}
p.five {color: hsla(0,0%,0%,0.2);}
```

Bringing the Colors Together

Table 2 presents an overview of some of the colors we've discussed. Note that there are some rows that do not contain shortened hexadecimal values. That happens in cases where the longer (six-digit) values cannot be shortened. For example, the value #880 expands to #888800, not #808000 (otherwise known as olive). Therefore, there is no shortened version of #808000, and the appropriate entry in the table is blank.

Table 2. Color equivalents

Color	Hexa-decimal	RGB Decimal	RGB Percentage	HSL
aqua	#00FFFF*	rgb(0,255,255)	rgb(0%,100%,100%)	hsl(180,100%,50%)
black	#000000*	rgb(0,0,0)	rgb(0%,0%,0%)	hsl(0,0%,0%)
blue	#0000FF*	rgb(0,0,255)	rgb(0%,0%,100%)	hsl(240,100%,50%)
fuchsia	#FF00FF*	rgb(255,0,255)	rgb(100%,0%,100%)	hsl(300,100%,50%)
gray	#808080	rgb(128,128,128)	rgb(50%,50%,50%)	hsl(0,0%,50%)
green	#008000	rgb(0,128,0)	rgb(0%,50%,0%)	hsl(120,100%,50%)
lime	#00FF00*	rgb(0,255,0)	rgb(0%,100%,0%)	hsl(120,100%,50%)
maroon	#800000	rgb(128,0,0)	rgb(50%,0%,0%)	hsl(0,100%,25%)
navy	#000080	rgb(0,0,128)	rgb(0%,0%,50%)	hsl(240,100%,25%)
olive	#808000	rgb(128,128,0)	rgb(50%,50%,0%)	hsl(60,100%,25%)
purple	#800080	rgb(128,0,128)	rgb(50%,0%,50%)	hsl(300,100%,25%)
red	#FF0000*	rgb(255,0,0)	rgb(100%,0%,0%)	hsl(0,100%,50%)
silver	#C0C0C0	rgb(192,192,192)	rgb(75%,75%,75%)	hsl(0,0%,80%)
teal	#008080	rgb(0,128,128)	rgb(0%,50%,50%)	hsl(180,100%,25%)
white	#FFFFFF*	rgb(255,255,255)	rgb(100%,100%,100%)	hsl(0,0%,100%)
yellow	#FFFF00*	rgb(255,255,0)	rgb(100%,100%,0%)	hsl(60,100%,50%)

* Can be represented using the "short-hex" pattern (e.g., #000).

Angles

Since we just finished talking about hue angles in HSL, this would be a good time to talk about angle units. Angles in general are represented as <*angle*>, which is a <*number*> followed by one of four unit types:

deg
> Degrees, of which there are 360 in a full circle.

grad
> Gradians, of which there are 400 in a full circle. Also known as "grades" or "gons."

rad
> Radians, of which there are 2π (approximately 6.28) in a full circle.

turn
> Turns, of which there is one in a full circle. This unit is mostly useful when animating a rotation and you wish to have it turn multiple times, such as 10turn to make it spin ten times. (Sadly, the pluralization turns is invalid, at least as of mid-2012.)

Table 3. Angle equivalents

Degrees	Gradians	Radians	Turns
45deg	50grad	0.785rad	0.125turn
90deg	100grad	1.571rad	0.25turn
180deg	200grad	3.142rad	0.5turn
270deg	300grad	4.712rad	0.75turn
360deg	400grad	6.283rad	1turn

Angle units are mostly used in 2D and 3D transforms, though they do appear in a few other places. Note that angle units are *not* used in HSL colors, where all hue angle values are *always* degrees and thus do not use the deg unit!

Time and Frequency

In cases where a property needs to express a period of time, the value is represented as *<time>* and is a *<number>* followed by either s (seconds) or ms (milliseconds.) Time values are most often used in transitions and animations, either to define durations or delays. The following two declarations will have exactly the same result.

```
a[href] {transition-duration: 2.4s;}
a[href] {transition-duration: 2400ms;}
```

Time values are also used in aural CSS, again to define durations or delays, but support for aural CSS is extremely limited as of this writing.

Another value type historically used in aural CSS is *<frequency>*, which is a *<number>* followed by either Hz (Hertz) or kHz (kiloHertz). As usual, the identifiers are case-insensitive, so Hz and hz are equivalent. The following two declarations will have exactly the same result:

```
h1 {pitch: 128hz;}
h1 {pitch: 0.128khz;}
```

Position

A *position value* is how you specify the placement of an origin image in a background area, and is represented as *<position>*. Its syntactical structure is rather complicated:

```
[
  [ left | center | right | top | bottom | <percentage> | <length> ] |
  [ left | center | right | <percentage> | <length> ]
  [ top | center | bottom | <percentage> | <length> ] |
  [ center | [ left | right ] [ <percentage> | <length> ]? ] &&
  [ center | [ top | bottom ] [ <percentage> | <length> ]? ]
]
```

That might seem a little nutty, but it's all down to the subtly complex patterns that this value type has to allow.

If you declare only one value, such as left or 25%, then a second value is set to center. Thus, left is the same as left center and 25% is the same as 25% center.

If you declare (either implicitly, as above, or explicitly) two values and the first one is a length or percentage, then it is *always* considered to be the horizontal value. This means that given 25% 35px, the 25% is a horizontal distance and the 35px is a vertical distance. If you swap them to say 35px 25%, then 35px is horizontal and 25% is vertical. This means that if you write 25% left or 35px right, the entire value is invalid because you have supplied two horizontal distances and no vertical distance. (Similarly, a value of right left or top bottom is invalid and will be ignored.) On the other hand, if you write left 25% or right 35px, there is no problem because you've given a horizontal distance (with the keyword) and a vertical distance (with the percentage or length).

If you declare four values (we'll deal with three just in a moment), then you must have two lengths or percentages, each of which is preceded by a keyword. In this case, each length or percentage specifies an offset distance, and each keyword defines the edge from which the offset is calculated. Thus, right 10px bottom 30px means an offset of 10 pixels to the left of the right edge, and an offset of 30 pixels up from the bottom edge. Similarly, top 50% left 35px means a 50 percent offset from the top and a 35-pixels-to-the-right offset from the left.

If you declare three values, the rules are the same as for four except the last offset is set to be zero (no offset). Thus right 20px top is the same as right 20px top 0.

Summary

Units and values cover a wide spectrum of areas, from length units to special keywords that describe effects (such as underline) to color units to the location of files (such as images). For the most part, units are the one area that user agents get almost totally correct, but it's those few little bugs and quirks that can get you. Navigator 4.x's failure to interpret relative URLs correctly, for example, has bedeviled many authors and led to an overreliance on absolute URLs. Colors are another area where user agents almost always do well, except for a few little quirks here and there. The vagaries of length units, however, far from being bugs, are an interesting problem for any author to tackle. These units all have their advantages and drawbacks, depending upon the circumstances in which they're used.

Color Equivalence Table

Color name	RGB Decimal	RGB Percentage	HSL	Hexadecimal	Short Hex
aliceblue	rgb(240,248,255)	rgb(94%,97%,100%)	hsl(208,100%,97%)	#F0F8FF	
antiquewhite	rgb(250,235,215)	rgb(98%,92%,84%)	hsl(34,78%,91%)	#FAEBD7	
aqua	rgb(0,255,255)	rgb(0%,100%,100%)	hsl(180,100%,50%)	#00FFFF	#0FF
aquamarine	rgb(127,255,212)	rgb(50%,100%,83%)	hsl(160,100%,75%)	#7FFFD4	
azure	rgb(240,255,255)	rgb(94%,100%,100%)	hsl(180,100%,97%)	#F0FFFF	
beige	rgb(245,245,220)	rgb(96%,96%,86%)	hsl(60,56%,91%)	#F5F5DC	
bisque	rgb(255,228,196)	rgb(100%,89%,77%)	hsl(33,100%,88%)	#FFE4C4	
black	rgb(0,0,0)	rgb(0%,0%,0%)	hsl(0,0%,0%)	#000000	#000
blanchedalmond	rgb(255,235,205)	rgb(100%,92%,80%)	hsl(36,100%,90%)	#FFEBCD	
blue	rgb(0,0,255)	rgb(0%,0%,100%)	hsl(240,100%,50%)	#0000FF	#00F
blueviolet	rgb(138,43,226)	rgb(54%,17%,89%)	hsl(271,76%,53%)	#8A2BE2	
brown	rgb(165,42,42)	rgb(65%,16%,16%)	hsl(0,59%,41%)	#A52A2A	
burlywood	rgb(222,184,135)	rgb(87%,72%,53%)	hsl(34,57%,70%)	#DEB887	
cadetblue	rgb(95,158,160)	rgb(37%,62%,63%)	hsl(182,25%,50%)	#5F9EA0	
chartreuse	rgb(127,255,0)	rgb(50%,100%,0%)	hsl(90,100%,50%)	#7FFF00	
chocolate	rgb(210,105,30)	rgb(82%,41%,12%)	hsl(25,75%,47%)	#D2691E	
coral	rgb(255,127,80)	rgb(100%,50%,31%)	hsl(16,100%,66%)	#FF7F50	
cornflowerblue	rgb(100,149,237)	rgb(39%,58%,93%)	hsl(219,79%,66%)	#6495ED	
cornsilk	rgb(255,248,220)	rgb(100%,97%,86%)	hsl(48,100%,93%)	#FFF8DC	
crimson	rgb(220,20,60)	rgb(86%,8%,24%)	hsl(348,83%,47%)	#DC143C	
cyan	rgb(0,255,255)	rgb(0%,100%,100%)	hsl(180,100%,50%)	#00FFFF	#0FF
darkblue	rgb(0,0,139)	rgb(0%,0%,55%)	hsl(240,100%,27%)	#00008B	

Color name	RGB Decimal	RGB Percentage	HSL	Hexa-decimal	Short Hex
darkcyan	rgb(0,139,139)	rgb(0%,55%,55%)	hsl(180,100%,27%)	#008B8B	
darkgoldenrod	rgb(184,134,11)	rgb(72%,53%,4%)	hsl(43,89%,38%)	#B8860B	
darkgray	rgb(169,169,169)	rgb(66%,66%,66%)	hsl(0,0%,66%)	#A9A9A9	
darkgreen	rgb(0,100,0)	rgb(0%,39%,0%)	hsl(120,100%,20%)	#006400	
darkgrey	rgb(169,169,169)	rgb(66%,66%,66%)	hsl(0,0%,66%)	#A9A9A9	
darkkhaki	rgb(189,183,107)	rgb(74%,72%,42%)	hsl(56,38%,58%)	#BDB76B	
darkmagenta	rgb(139,0,139)	rgb(55%,0%,55%)	hsl(300,100%,27%)	#8B008B	
darkolivegreen	rgb(85,107,47)	rgb(33%,42%,18%)	hsl(82,39%,30%)	#556B2F	
darkorange	rgb(255,140,0)	rgb(100%,55%,0%)	hsl(33,100%,50%)	#FF8C00	
darkorchid	rgb(153,50,204)	rgb(60%,20%,80%)	hsl(280,61%,50%)	#9932CC	
darkred	rgb(139,0,0)	rgb(55%,0%,0%)	hsl(0,100%,27%)	#8B0000	
darksalmon	rgb(233,150,122)	rgb(91%,59%,48%)	hsl(15,72%,70%)	#E9967A	
darkseagreen	rgb(143,188,143)	rgb(56%,74%,56%)	hsl(120,25%,65%)	#8FBC8F	
darkslateblue	rgb(72,61,139)	rgb(28%,24%,55%)	hsl(248,39%,39%)	#483D8B	
darkslategray	rgb(47,79,79)	rgb(18%,31%,31%)	hsl(180,25%,25%)	#2F4F4F	
darkslategrey	rgb(47,79,79)	rgb(18%,31%,31%)	hsl(180,25%,25%)	#2F4F4F	
darkturquoise	rgb(0,206,209)	rgb(0%,81%,82%)	hsl(181,100%,41%)	#00CED1	
darkviolet	rgb(148,0,211)	rgb(58%,0%,83%)	hsl(282,100%,41%)	#9400D3	
deeppink	rgb(255,20,147)	rgb(100%,8%,58%)	hsl(328,100%,54%)	#FF1493	
deepskyblue	rgb(0,191,255)	rgb(0%,75%,100%)	hsl(195,100%,50%)	#00BFFF	
dimgray	rgb(105,105,105)	rgb(41%,41%,41%)	hsl(0,0%,41%)	#696969	
dimgrey	rgb(105,105,105)	rgb(41%,41%,41%)	hsl(0,0%,41%)	#696969	

Color name	RGB Decimal	RGB Percentage	HSL	Hexa-decimal	Short Hex
dodgerblue	rgb(30,144,255)	rgb(12%,56%,100%)	hsl(210,100%,56%)	#1E90FF	
firebrick	rgb(178,34,34)	rgb(70%,13%,13%)	hsl(0,68%,42%)	#B22222	
floralwhite	rgb(255,250,240)	rgb(100%,98%,94%)	hsl(40,100%,97%)	#FFFAF0	
forestgreen	rgb(34,139,34)	rgb(13%,55%,13%)	hsl(120,61%,34%)	#228B22	
fuchsia	rgb(255,0,255)	rgb(100%,0%,100%)	hsl(300,100%,50%)	#FF00FF	#F0F
gainsboro	rgb(220,220,220)	rgb(86%,86%,86%)	hsl(0,0%,86%)	#DCDCDC	
ghostwhite	rgb(248,248,255)	rgb(97%,97%,100%)	hsl(240,100%,99%)	#F8F8FF	
gold	rgb(255,215,0)	rgb(100%,84%,0%)	hsl(51,100%,50%)	#FFD700	
goldenrod	rgb(218,165,32)	rgb(85%,65%,13%)	hsl(43,74%,49%)	#DAA520	
gray	rgb(128,128,128)	rgb(50%,50%,50%)	hsl(0,0%,50%)	#808080	
green	rgb(0,128,0)	rgb(0%,50%,0%)	hsl(120,100%,25%)	#008000	
greenyellow	rgb(173,255,47)	rgb(68%,100%,18%)	hsl(84,100%,59%)	#ADFF2F	
grey	rgb(128,128,128)	rgb(50%,50%,50%)	hsl(0,0%,50%)	#808080	
honeydew	rgb(240,255,240)	rgb(94%,100%,94%)	hsl(120,100%,97%)	#F0FFF0	
hotpink	rgb(255,105,180)	rgb(100%,41%,71%)	hsl(330,100%,71%)	#FF69B4	
indianred	rgb(205,92,92)	rgb(80%,36%,36%)	hsl(0,53%,58%)	#CD5C5C	
indigo	rgb(75,0,130)	rgb(29%,0%,51%)	hsl(275,100%,25%)	#4B0082	
ivory	rgb(255,255,240)	rgb(100%,100%,94%)	hsl(60,100%,97%)	#FFFFF0	
khaki	rgb(240,230,140)	rgb(94%,90%,55%)	hsl(54,77%,75%)	#F0E68C	
lavender	rgb(230,230,250)	rgb(90%,90%,98%)	hsl(240,67%,94%)	#E6E6FA	
lavenderblush	rgb(255,240,245)	rgb(100%,94%,96%)	hsl(340,100%,97%)	#FFF0F5	
lawngreen	rgb(124,252,0)	rgb(49%,99%,0%)	hsl(90,100%,49%)	#7CFC00	

Color name	RGB Decimal	RGB Percentage	HSL	Hexa-decimal	Short Hex
lemonchiffon	rgb(255,250,205)	rgb(100%,98%,80%)	hsl(54,100%,90%)	#FFFACD	
lightblue	rgb(173,216,230)	rgb(68%,85%,90%)	hsl(195,53%,79%)	#ADD8E6	
lightcoral	rgb(240,128,128)	rgb(94%,50%,50%)	hsl(0,79%,72%)	#F08080	
lightcyan	rgb(224,255,255)	rgb(88%,100%,100%)	hsl(180,100%,94%)	#E0FFFF	
lightgoldenrodyellow	rgb(250,250,210)	rgb(98%,98%,82%)	hsl(60,80%,90%)	#FAFAD2	
lightgray	rgb(211,211,211)	rgb(83%,83%,83%)	hsl(0,0%,83%)	#D3D3D3	
lightgreen	rgb(144,238,144)	rgb(56%,93%,56%)	hsl(120,73%,75%)	#90EE90	
lightgrey	rgb(211,211,211)	rgb(83%,83%,83%)	hsl(0,0%,83%)	#D3D3D3	
lightpink	rgb(255,182,193)	rgb(100%,71%,76%)	hsl(351,100%,86%)	#FFB6C1	
lightsalmon	rgb(255,160,122)	rgb(100%,63%,48%)	hsl(17,100%,74%)	#FFA07A	
lightseagreen	rgb(32,178,170)	rgb(13%,70%,67%)	hsl(177,70%,41%)	#20B2AA	
lightskyblue	rgb(135,206,250)	rgb(53%,81%,98%)	hsl(203,92%,75%)	#87CEFA	
lightslategray	rgb(119,136,153)	rgb(47%,53%,60%)	hsl(210,14%,53%)	#778899	#789
lightslategrey	rgb(119,136,153)	rgb(47%,53%,60%)	hsl(210,14%,53%)	#778899	#789
lightsteelblue	rgb(176,196,222)	rgb(69%,77%,87%)	hsl(214,41%,78%)	#B0C4DE	
lightyellow	rgb(255,255,224)	rgb(100%,100%,88%)	hsl(60,100%,94%)	#FFFFE0	
lime	rgb(0,255,0)	rgb(0%,100%,0%)	hsl(120,100%,50%)	#00FF00	#0F0
limegreen	rgb(50,205,50)	rgb(20%,80%,20%)	hsl(120,61%,50%)	#32CD32	
linen	rgb(250,240,230)	rgb(98%,94%,90%)	hsl(30,67%,94%)	#FAF0E6	
magenta	rgb(255,0,255)	rgb(100%,0%,100%)	hsl(300,100%,50%)	#FF00FF	#F0F
maroon	rgb(128,0,0)	rgb(50%,0%,0%)	hsl(0,100%,25%)	#800000	
mediumaquamarine	rgb(102,205,170)	rgb(40%,80%,67%)	hsl(160,51%,60%)	#66CDAA	

Color name	RGB Decimal	RGB Percentage	HSL	Hexa-decimal	Short Hex
mediumblue	rgb(0,0,205)	rgb(0%,0%,80%)	hsl(240,100%,40%)	#0000CD	
mediumorchid	rgb(186,85,211)	rgb(73%,33%,83%)	hsl(288,59%,58%)	#BA55D3	
mediumpurple	rgb(147,112,219)	rgb(58%,44%,86%)	hsl(260,60%,65%)	#9370DB	
mediumseagreen	rgb(60,179,113)	rgb(24%,70%,44%)	hsl(147,50%,47%)	#3CB371	
mediumslateblue	rgb(123,104,238)	rgb(48%,41%,93%)	hsl(249,80%,67%)	#7B68EE	
mediumspringgreen	rgb(0,250,154)	rgb(0%,98%,60%)	hsl(157,100%,49%)	#00FA9A	
mediumturquoise	rgb(72,209,204)	rgb(28%,82%,80%)	hsl(178,60%,55%)	#48D1CC	
mediumvioletred	rgb(199,21,133)	rgb(78%,8%,52%)	hsl(322,81%,43%)	#C71585	
midnightblue	rgb(25,25,112)	rgb(10%,10%,44%)	hsl(240,64%,27%)	#191970	
mintcream	rgb(245,255,250)	rgb(96%,100%,98%)	hsl(150,100%,98%)	#F5FFFA	
mistyrose	rgb(255,228,225)	rgb(100%,89%,88%)	hsl(6,100%,94%)	#FFE4E1	
moccasin	rgb(255,228,181)	rgb(100%,89%,71%)	hsl(38,100%,85%)	#FFE4B5	
navajowhite	rgb(255,222,173)	rgb(100%,87%,68%)	hsl(36,100%,84%)	#FFDEAD	
navy	rgb(0,0,128)	rgb(0%,0%,50%)	hsl(240,100%,25%)	#000080	
oldlace	rgb(253,245,230)	rgb(99%,96%,90%)	hsl(39,85%,95%)	#FDF5E6	
olive	rgb(128,128,0)	rgb(50%,50%,0%)	hsl(60,100%,25%)	#808000	
olivedrab	rgb(107,142,35)	rgb(42%,56%,14%)	hsl(80,60%,35%)	#6B8E23	
orange	rgb(255,165,0)	rgb(100%,65%,0%)	hsl(39,100%,50%)	#FFA500	
orangered	rgb(255,69,0)	rgb(100%,27%,0%)	hsl(16,100%,50%)	#FF4500	
orchid	rgb(218,112,214)	rgb(85%,44%,84%)	hsl(302,59%,65%)	#DA70D6	
palegoldenrod	rgb(238,232,170)	rgb(93%,91%,67%)	hsl(55,67%,80%)	#EEE8AA	
palegreen	rgb(152,251,152)	rgb(60%,98%,60%)	hsl(120,93%,79%)	#98FB98	

Color name	RGB Decimal	RGB Percentage	HSL	Hexa-decimal	Short Hex
paleturquoise	rgb(175,238,238)	rgb(69%,93%,93%)	hsl(180,65%,81%)	#AFEEEE	
palevioletred	rgb(219,112,147)	rgb(86%,44%,58%)	hsl(340,60%,65%)	#DB7093	
papayawhip	rgb(255,239,213)	rgb(100%,94%,84%)	hsl(37,100%,92%)	#FFEFD5	
peachpuff	rgb(255,218,185)	rgb(100%,85%,73%)	hsl(28,100%,86%)	#FFDAB9	
peru	rgb(205,133,63)	rgb(80%,52%,25%)	hsl(30,59%,53%)	#CD853F	
pink	rgb(255,192,203)	rgb(100%,75%,80%)	hsl(350,100%,88%)	#FFC0CB	
plum	rgb(221,160,221)	rgb(87%,63%,87%)	hsl(300,47%,75%)	#DDA0DD	
powderblue	rgb(176,224,230)	rgb(69%,88%,90%)	hsl(187,52%,80%)	#B0E0E6	
purple	rgb(128,0,128)	rgb(50%,0%,50%)	hsl(300,100%,25%)	#800080	
red	rgb(255,0,0)	rgb(100%,0%,0%)	hsl(0,100%,50%)	#FF0000	#F00
rosybrown	rgb(188,143,143)	rgb(74%,56%,56%)	hsl(0,25%,65%)	#BC8F8F	
royalblue	rgb(65,105,225)	rgb(25%,41%,88%)	hsl(225,73%,57%)	#4169E1	
saddlebrown	rgb(139,69,19)	rgb(55%,27%,7%)	hsl(25,76%,31%)	#8B4513	
salmon	rgb(250,128,114)	rgb(98%,50%,45%)	hsl(6,93%,71%)	#FA8072	
sandybrown	rgb(244,164,96)	rgb(96%,64%,38%)	hsl(28,87%,67%)	#F4A460	
seagreen	rgb(46,139,87)	rgb(18%,55%,34%)	hsl(146,50%,36%)	#2E8B57	
seashell	rgb(255,245,238)	rgb(100%,96%,93%)	hsl(25,100%,97%)	#FFF5EE	
sienna	rgb(160,82,45)	rgb(63%,32%,18%)	hsl(19,56%,40%)	#A0522D	
silver	rgb(192,192,192)	rgb(75%,75%,75%)	hsl(0,0%,75%)	#C0C0C0	
skyblue	rgb(135,206,235)	rgb(53%,81%,92%)	hsl(197,71%,73%)	#87CEEB	
slateblue	rgb(106,90,205)	rgb(42%,35%,80%)	hsl(248,53%,58%)	#6A5ACD	
slategray	rgb(112,128,144)	rgb(44%,50%,56%)	hsl(210,13%,50%)	#708090	

Color name	RGB Decimal	RGB Percentage	HSL	Hexa-decimal	Short Hex
slategrey	rgb(112,128,144)	rgb(44%,50%,56%)	hsl(210,13%,50%)	#708090	
snow	rgb(255,250,250)	rgb(100%,98%,98%)	hsl(0,100%,99%)	#FFFAFA	
springgreen	rgb(0,255,127)	rgb(0%,100%,50%)	hsl(150,100%,50%)	#00FF7F	
steelblue	rgb(70,130,180)	rgb(27%,51%,71%)	hsl(207,44%,49%)	#4682B4	
tan	rgb(210,180,140)	rgb(82%,71%,55%)	hsl(34,44%,69%)	#D2B48C	
teal	rgb(0,128,128)	rgb(0%,50%,50%)	hsl(180,100%,25%)	#008080	
thistle	rgb(216,191,216)	rgb(85%,75%,85%)	hsl(300,24%,80%)	#D8BFD8	
tomato	rgb(255,99,71)	rgb(100%,39%,28%)	hsl(9,100%,64%)	#FF6347	
turquoise	rgb(64,224,208)	rgb(25%,88%,82%)	hsl(174,72%,56%)	#40E0D0	
violet	rgb(238,130,238)	rgb(93%,51%,93%)	hsl(300,76%,72%)	#EE82EE	
wheat	rgb(245,222,179)	rgb(96%,87%,70%)	hsl(39,77%,83%)	#F5DEB3	
white	rgb(255,255,255)	rgb(100%,100%,100%)	hsl(0,0%,100%)	#FFFFFF	#FFF
whitesmoke	rgb(245,245,245)	rgb(96%,96%,96%)	hsl(0,0%,96%)	#F5F5F5	
yellow	rgb(255,255,0)	rgb(100%,100%,0%)	hsl(60,100%,50%)	#FFFF00	#FF0
yellowgreen	rgb(154,205,50)	rgb(60%,80%,20%)	hsl(80,61%,50%)	#9ACD32	

About the Author

Eric A. Meyer has been working with the Web since late 1993 and is an internationally recognized expert on the subjects of HTML, CSS, and web standards. A widely read author, he is a past member of the CSS&FP Working Group and was the primary creator of the W3C's CSS1 Test Suite. In 2006, Eric was inducted into the International Academy of Digital Arts and Sciences for "international recognition on the topics of HTML and CSS" and helping to "inform excellence and efficiency on the Web."

Eric is currently the principal founder at Complex Spiral Consulting, which counts among its clients a wide variety of corporations, educational institutions, and government agencies. He is also, along with Jeffrey Zeldman, co-founder of An Event Apart ("The design conference for people who make websites"), and he speaks regularly at that conference as well as many others. Eric lives with his family in Cleveland, Ohio, which is a much nicer city than you've been led to believe. A historian by training and inclination, he enjoys a good meal whenever he can and considers almost every form of music to be worthwhile.

Get even more for your money.

Join the O'Reilly Community, and register the O'Reilly books you own. It's free, and you'll get:

- $4.99 ebook upgrade offer
- 40% upgrade offer on O'Reilly print books
- Membership discounts on books and events
- Free lifetime updates to ebooks and videos
- Multiple ebook formats, DRM FREE
- Participation in the O'Reilly community
- Newsletters
- Account management
- 100% Satisfaction Guarantee

Signing up is easy:

1. Go to: oreilly.com/go/register
2. Create an O'Reilly login.
3. Provide your address.
4. Register your books.

Note: English-language books only

To order books online:
oreilly.com/store

For questions about products or an order:
orders@oreilly.com

To sign up to get topic-specific email announcements and/or news about upcoming books, conferences, special offers, and new technologies:
elists@oreilly.com

For technical questions about book content:
booktech@oreilly.com

To submit new book proposals to our editors:
proposals@oreilly.com

O'Reilly books are available in multiple DRM-free ebook formats. For more information:
oreilly.com/ebooks

O'REILLY®

Spreading the knowledge of innovators | oreilly.com

Have it your way.